TRAILWAYS BUSES
1936 THROUGH 2001
PHOTO ARCHIVE

William A. Luke

Iconografix
Photo Archive Series

Iconografix
PO Box 446
Hudson, Wisconsin 54016 USA

Library of Congress Card Number: 00-132388

ISBN 1-58388-029-1

00 01 02 03 04 05 06 5 4 3 2 1

Printed in the United States of America

Cover and book design by Shawn Glidden

Copy editing by Dylan Frautschi

Book Proposals

Iconografix is a publishing company specializing in books for transportation enthusiasts. We publish in a number of different areas, including Automobiles, Auto Racing, Buses, Construction Equipment, Emergency Equipment, Farming Equipment, Railroads & Trucks. The Iconografix imprint is constantly growing and expanding into new subject areas.

Authors, editors, and knowledgeable enthusiasts in the field of transportation history are invited to contact the Editorial Department at Iconografix, Inc., PO Box 446, Hudson, WI 54016.

Table of Contents

ACKNOWLEDGMENTS

Photographs in this book are from the bus history library of the author, William A. Luke, unless noted as photo credits from other individuals and organizations

The following persons and organizations were very helpful in providing information that has made this book possible.

Tom Jones, Librarian, Motor Bus Society, Clark, New Jersey

Donald Coffin, bus historian, Hawley, Pennsylvania

Paul Leger, President, Bus History Association, Halifax, Nova Scotia

Gale C. Ellsworth, President/CEO Trailways Transportation System, Fairfax, Virginia

Also various members of the Trailways Transportation System nationwide

Special mention should also be made to acknowledge the late Tom Van De Grift, who for a number of years, presented many photographs (some of which are used in this book) to the library of William A. Luke and others.

FOREWORD

You're about to traverse more than six decades of travel with Trailways, a name that has left an indelible imprint on public transportation in the twentieth century and is poised to make global tread marks in a new millennium.

I know you'll enjoy the journey through these adventure-filled archives of more than 100 vintage photographs and captions, carefully researched, compiled and written by William A. Luke. A former editor/publisher of *Bus Ride* Magazine and founder of the Buses International Association, Mr. Luke has masterfully applied his extensive experience in the motorcoach industry to bring Trailways' legacy to life. With each turn of the page, he reveals the exciting story of how Trailways has trekked over smooth and bumpy roads to help shape the travel and transportation industry.

Trailways has an admirable heritage, driven by a strong commitment to the spirit of independence. A trip back to 1936 reveals five independent bus operators forming National Trailways Bus System to protect and support family-run bus companies from industry giants during the Great Depression. Through decades of travel, Trailways and its blazing, crimson insignia earned an international reputation as one of the most respected brand names in motorcoach transportation. Trailways became synonymous with safe, dependable, first-class transportation delivered with friendly service to ensure a pleasant, comfortable ride.

When Trailways started its first engine many years ago, the organization represented the first of its kind to serve independent motorcoach owners and operators. Once legendary for its intercity scheduled-route travel, it has expanded to include charter and tour members, and has begun to forge inter-modal alliances with other ground, air, rail, and sea transportation and travel organizations. Today, Trailways is blazing new trails, building a powerful, world-class brand through the efforts of independently owned member companies, partners and supporters committed to offering the public the best choice in travel and transportation services. Much has changed for Trailways as it has stretched across the horizon of a new millennium to explore new markets and global opportunities in order to provide unparalleled member services and cutting-edge, convenient travel options for consumers. Yet its fundamental values are enduring: independence combined with a commitment to support and help one another succeed in providing a safe, dependable, comfortable, and pleasurable travel experience.

William Luke has captured the essence of Trailways beautifully in this remarkable book. He has enabled us to reminisce while celebrating Trailways' transformation into a global travel and transportation and industry trailblazer. Thank you, Mr. Luke. I also want to thank Trailways' many dedicated members and friends who led us to our past successes and can join us in an extraordinarily successful future.

Gale Ellsworth
President/Chief Executive Officer
Trailways Transportation System, Inc.
Fairfax, Virginia, USA
www.trailways.com
or www.TravelByBus.com

INTRODUCTION

Trailways has been an important part of transportation in America since 1936. Today, Trailways has changed but continues with emphasis on a broader scope for transportation globally. One of the original goals was for members to cooperate and create the teamwork that would promote growth in travel. That goal continues. Team Trailways has become the catch phrase.

There has been considerable change in the bus industry since Trailways, originally known as the National Trailways Bus System (NTBS), began. Challenges, especially in the latter part of the 20th century, may have seemed insurmountable; but Trailways and its members adapted to change, and Trailways continued to grow. The cooperation and exchange of ideas and information among members has been noteworthy. Trailways has had a rich, colorful history.

In 1935, representatives of five bus companies held a meeting in Detroit. At this meeting there were discussions about starting an organization of independent bus companies. This first planning team included: Frank Martz, Sr., of Frank Martz Coach Company, Wilkes-Barre, Pennsylvania; Hy Moore of Safeway Lines Inc., Chicago; A. E. Greenleaf of Santa Fe Trails Transportation Company, Wichita, Kansas; Paul Neff of Missouri Pacific Stages, St. Louis, Missouri; and I. B. James of Burlington Transportation Company, Chicago. The 1935 meeting led to a February 5, 1936 meeting in the office of H. W. Stewart, then general manager of Burlington Transportation Company, and at that time the National Trailways Bus System was officially formed. Chicago was selected as the headquarters.

New members were encouraged, and at the end of 1937, Trailways had 16 member companies. By March 1940 there were 34 members.

In many cases prior to the formation of Trailways, each bus company operated from its own bus terminal especially in large cities. An initial Trailways goal was to have one terminal in all larger cities. Chicago was an important hub for Trailways members, and it wasn't long before a Trailways terminal was established there.

New York City was another hub. When Adirondack Transit Lines joined Trailways, the Dixie Terminal in New York City, which Adirondack controlled, became that important hub. The Dixie Terminal served Trailways members until 1950, when the large Port Authority Bus Terminal opened and Trailways companies began using that terminal.

Various standards were recommended. Crimson and cream were the colors chosen, and buses appeared everywhere showing the Trailways colors. A symbol using the outline of the United States was adopted along with "hobo" style lettering.

National advertising began. Full-page, full-color advertisements began appearing in many consumer magazines. Trailways was on the move.

Although Trailways companies had a variety of bus types, the symbol, colors and Trailways name readily identified the nationwide Trailways. ACF-Brill Motors Company had stock in a number of Trailways companies, therefore ACF buses were dominant and considered the flagship buses for Trailways in the 1930s and 1940s.

Tourism has been important for the bus industry. Trailways recognized this from the beginning, and in 1942, the Interstate Commerce Commission issued one of the first tour brokers permits to Trailways. This resulted in the National Trailways Travel Bureau.

During World War II, Trailways buses moved troops and defense workers in great numbers. Many military establishments were in the states served by Trailways members. The buses and personnel of Trailways companies performed beyond the normal expectations to help the war effort.

After World War II a big change occurred affecting the Trailways. In 1946, Continental Bus System was formed through an initial merger of two companies and eventually involved a number of Trailways members. All merged companies continued Trailways membership, but they were under the Continental Trailways name.

Later, Continental Trailways had a couple of ownership turnovers and changed its name to Trailways, Inc.

The bus industry was changing in the 1970s. The formation of the National Railroad Passenger Corporation (Amtrak) and the subsidized competition it presented, the fuel crisis, deregulation, and the insurance crisis brought about concerns not only to Trailways but also the entire bus industry.

Then, Trailways, Inc., fell into bad times and was acquired by Greyhound Lines. The nationwide bus competition virtually ended. Trailways companies in the East remained strong, and there were a number of new members. Trailways was adapting to change and surviving in a manner different than the original direction.

The official name now has become the Trailways Transportation System, Inc., and the logo represents the globe. In other words, it is not only motorcoach transportation or only the United States; but the focus is now international and on intermodal transportation.

Statistically, there are more than 50 transportation companies in the renewed Trailways organization. Because a new Charter and Tour Division of Team Trailways has been established, there are a greater number of companies in this category, and it is growing.

Trailways' regular route companies continue to be strong with more than 500 destinations served and with more than 1,000 buses.

Trailways also has associate members, which include motorcoach manufacturers and other companies supplying products and services to the transportation members. In addition, there are affiliate members whose mission is to support the transportation and tourism industries.

The Trailways Transportation System, Inc. continues to be one of the largest organizations of its type with members from independent companies. They share a common interest and ambitious goals.

It is interesting to note that one of the Trailways slogans today is, "See the world the way it was meant to be seen...at scenery level." In the 1950s it was "See America at Scenery Level."

One of the most important Trailways commitments today, as it was in the beginning, is to provide the best possible service to the traveling public.

Santa Fe Trail Transportation Company was originally the Southern Kansas Stage Lines, a sizable bus line in the 1920s. The Atchison Topeka & Santa Fe Railway became interested and acquired the company in the 1930s. In 1936 the Santa Fe Trail System became one of the founders of the National Trailways Bus System. At that time it was the largest segment of the system and operated more than 10,000 route miles. There were many small feeder lines to the Santa Fe Trail System, and small buses like this 1934 Chevrolet were used.

De Luxe Motor Stages, which operated mainly in Illinois and between Chicago and St. Louis, began in the early 1930s. It joined the National Trailways Bus System in 1941 as De Luxe Trailways. In 1935 it operated this 26-passenger DMX, a small intercity bus built by the Dittmar Manufacturing Company in Harvey, Illinois.

Red Ball Bus Company of Enid, Oklahoma, was a sizable bus company in 1936 when this Beck-bodied Chevrolet was acquired. Red Ball later changed owners and moved to Oklahoma City. The name became Mid Continent Coaches about the same time it joined the National Trailways Bus System. An important through route was operated between Oklahoma City and Denver. In the 1980s and 1990s virtually all the communities in Oklahoma which had service by Red Ball and Mid Continent lost regular intercity bus service.

Prior to joining the National Trailways Bus System, Santa Fe Transportation System operated a number of small 16-passenger Flxible Airway buses. These buses were built on Chevrolet truck chassis. This one was a 1934 model. Santa Fe was one of the founding National Trailways Bus System members in 1936.

Carolina Coach Company of Raleigh, North Carolina, added four ACF model H-9-P buses to its fleet in 1936. The company was more than 10 years old at that time. In four years it was to become a member of the National Trailways Bus System. Carolina was important for Trailways because it was midway on the bus routes between the large metropolitan areas of the East and Florida.

Rio Grande Motorway, a subsidiary of the Rio Grande and Western Railway, had a history of bus operation dating back to the early 1920s. The company joined the National Trailways Bus System in 1936, two months after the organization was founded. A number of the buses in the Rio Grande fleet, like this Yellow Coach Z-250 Model 649, were repainted in Trailways livery.

At the time when Santa Fe Trail Transportation Company with four other bus companies formed the National Trailways Bus System in 1936, Santa Fe was operating Yellow Coach Z-250 Model 843 buses. Note that the Trailways name had not been used on the buses, but the Trailways emblem had been applied. Santa Fe had extensive routes from St. Louis and Kansas City to the West Coast. Santa Fe also had an important route between Los Angeles and San Francisco.

Burlington Transportation Company, a subsidiary of the Chicago Burlington and Quincy Railroad, was incorporated in 1929. In 1936 when the National Trailways Bus System was formed, Burlington Transportation Company was one of the founding members. At the time Burlington was operating Yellow Coach Model 788 Z-250 streamliner buses.

Lincoln Trailways operated between Chicago and Pittsburgh via Fort Wayne, and Columbus in 1936 when it joined the National Trailways Bus System. The bus pictured here is a Lincoln Trailways Yellow Coach Z-255 Model 843 Streamliner acquired in 1936.

Missouri Pacific Transportation Co., a subsidiary of the Missouri Pacific Railroad, was formed in 1928. The company was one of the original National Trailways Bus System members. In 1936, at the time Missouri Pacific joined Trailways, 19 Yellow Coach Z-250 Model 843 buses were acquired. Three of these buses are pictured here.

The year before Burlington Transportation Company became one of the founding members of the National Trailways Bus System it bought ten Yellow Coach Z-250 Model 843 buses. They were later repainted in the Burlington "pin stripe" paint scheme of crimson and cream colors. *Don Coffin Collection*

In 1936, when the National Trailways Bus System was formed, Santa Fe Trailways, one of the original members, took delivery of these H9P ACF buses. This was the start of a trend of Trailways companies using ACF buses, which continued until ACF ceased building buses in 1953.

This ACF Model H-15-P, bus was purchased before Missouri Kansas & Oklahoma Coach Lines (MK & O) joined the National Trailways Bus System in 1936. The bus could seat 26 passengers and had a 115-horsepower Hall Scott engine. This bus had a transit style body which was adapted for intercity use. MK & O operated a main route at that time between St. Louis and Oklahoma City and had several local routes.

Missouri, Kansas & Oklahoma Trailways was one of the earlier members of the National Trailways Bus System. The famous Route 66 between St. Louis and Oklahoma City formed an important link for Trailways service to the East at St. Louis and to the West at Oklahoma City. In 1937 and 1938 Missouri, Kansas & Oklahoma Trailways acquired 18 Yellow Coach Model 732 buses like the one pictured here.

Safeway Trailways was one of the original members of the National Trailways Bus System when it began in 1936. The original Safe Way line was between New York and Chicago. The company went into receivership in 1938 and Northern Trailways assumed the route. It is unknown whether this 20-passenger Flxible Clipper ever entered Safe Way service when it was introduced in 1937. These small Flxible Clippers were mounted on Chevrolet Truck chassis.

In 1938, two years after it joined the National Trailways Bus System, Rio Grande Motorway purchased two ACF 37P buses, seating 37 passengers. At that time, Rio Grande had important routes between Denver and Salt Lake City and Pueblo, Colorado, and Salt Lake City. There were also a number of connecting lines throughout Colorado. In 1948 Rio Grande Trailways became a subsidiary of the Transcontinental Bus System and assumed the name Continental Rocky Mountain Lines.

Santa Fe Trailways operated night coach service using Pickwick Sleeper buses between Kansas City and Los Angeles in 1935. Santa Fe had eight of these buses, which were originally owned and operated by Columbia-Pacific Nite Coach for a brief time. The service ended when World War II began and sleeper bus service was never reinstated.

24

Burlington Trailways was one of the first long-distance bus companies to operate diesel buses. In 1939 Burlington acquired 21 Yellow Coach Model 743 buses. They had 6-71 General Motors diesel engines, and air conditioning was also featured. Burlington named the buses DieseLiners and had considerable promotion for the service with DieseLiners.

Blueway Trailways had its beginning in the early 1920s with several pioneer bus companies. They joined to become Blue Way Lines in 1932, and joined the National Trailways Bus System in 1938 when this Flxible 25-CR-8 was added to the fleet. Blueway became Trailways of New England.

Tri State Coaches of Shreveport, Louisiana, was one of the larger Trailways companies in the South. It became a member of the National Trailways Bus System in 1940. Then, in 1943, Tri State bought Bowen Motor Coaches (then also a Trailways Company) which brought about the formation of Continental Bus System. Tri State was operating a number of air-conditioned, 29-passenger Flxible Clippers in 1940.

By 1940 Panhandle Stages of Amarillo, Texas, had six Flxible buses in its fleet including this 25BR140B Buick-engined, 25-passenger Flxible Clipper. Panhandle, which joined the National Trailways Bus System in 1936, had a key Trailways connecting route between Oklahoma City and Amarillo. There were also other Panhandle feeder routes.

In 1936 Gar Wood Industries, a boat and truck builder in Michigan, began building a small bus featuring a welded steel framework. In 1939 General American Transportation Corporation bought the Gar Wood bus-building operation and built the Gar Wood-type bus for several years. Yankee Trailways, which had this Gar Wood Aerocoach, operated it on its line between Chicago and Indianapolis in 1940. Indianapolis and Southeastern Trailways later acquired the line.

Bowen Motor Coaches was formed in 1937 and joined the National Trailways Bus System in 1940. It was one of the principal parts of the Transcontinental Bus System (Continental Trailways) in 1947. Bowen had very choice routes in Texas: Dallas, Amarillo, and Dallas-Houston. Pictured here in 1938 is a 29-passenger Flxible Clipper. Different from most Clippers of the day were the rounded side windows. The bus was also air-conditioned.

Yellow Coach introduced a small intercity Model 1209 bus in 1939. To compete with the many small buses being marketed at that time, Yellow Coach called these 25-passenger buses Cruiserettes. Missouri Pacific had 19, which were used on a number of the small feeder routes of the company.

Burlington Trailways had a number of small lines connecting to its longer routes. To serve these small routes Burlington bought five Kalamazoo Pony Cruiser buses in 1939. The buses were used primarily in South Dakota's Black Hills. The Pony Cruisers were built on Ford truck chassis with 95-horsepower Ford V-8 engines and had seating for 13 passengers.

Soon after the National Trailways Bus System was formed one of the new members was the Peoria Rockford Bus Company. It adapted the name Central Trailways. Peoria Rockford Bus Company began serving the two Illinois cities in its name. When it joined Trailways it had extended its route north to Milwaukee, Wisconsin. Changes took place in the 1980s and 1990s and Peoria Rockford began service between Rockford and Chicago's O'Hare Airport. Other regular-route services were discontinued, as well as Trailways membership. Pictured here are two 25CK-42 Flxible Clippers labeled Central Trailways. These were the pride of the fleet at that time. These Flxible Clippers had Chevrolet engines.

Crescent Stages operated a number of important routes in Alabama and Tennessee when it joined the National Trailways Bus System in 1939 and became Crescent Trailways. In 1941 these four Flxible Clipper Model 25-CR-41 buses were purchased. Crescent Trailways was purchased by Transcontinental Bus System (Continental) in 1953.

Flxible Clipper buses were very popular with many small and medium size bus companies in the late 1930s and 1940s. This 29-passenger Buick-powered Flxible Clipper was in service for Queen City Trailways. Not only did this bus have the National Trailways Bus System emblem, but it also had the special Queen City shield emblem just behind the front wheel.

Frisco Transportation Company of Springfield, Missouri, a subsidiary of the St. Louis & San Francisco Railway, was a member of the National Trailways Bus System for a few years. It operated a number of routes through southern Missouri in the 1940s and 1950s. Pictured is one of Frisco Trailways' Beck Steeliner buses with a Chevrolet front engine.

The 1940 Kalamazoo Pony Cruiser was changed from the original model introduced two years before. The 1940 model was mounted on a heavier Ford truck chassis. Burlington Trailways added five of these Pony Cruisers in 1940 to serve small feeder lines.

Most Trailways companies usually had their full name displayed on their buses. However, this 1941 Flxible Clipper 25-CR-41 just had National Trailways. It was one of the buses operated by Smoky Mountain Trailways. Smoky Mountain had main routes between Asheville, North Carolina, and Atlanta, Georgia, via Chattanooga, Tennessee, as well as another Asheville-Atlanta route.

Denver-Colorado Springs-Pueblo Motorways joined the National Trailways Bus System in 1936 along with other Colorado bus companies, and became known as Denver-Colorado Springs-Pueblo Trailways. In 1938 three ACF 37P buses were purchased. The buses were painted in attractive cream and red and carried the Trailways emblem.

Burlington Trailways had a small bus terminal in St. Joseph, Missouri. It also served schedules of Santa Fe Trailways and Jefferson Transportation Co. In this picture taken about 1940, customers were invited to have a look at the new air-conditioned Santa Fe Trailways ACF Bus, model 37PB, on the right. A Burlington Trailways Yellow Coach Model 743 is shown on the left.

Interurban Transportation Company operated a very important route in Louisiana. As a result, this Shreveport to New Orleans route connected with the Tri State Trailways services to the North. Interurban joined the National Trailways Bus System in 1940. At that time ACF 37PB buses were being operated.

Safeway Trailways, one of the originating Trailways member companies, went into receivership. Virginia Stage Lines, a Trailways member, came to the rescue and a new Safeway Trailways was the result in 1938. The route was between Washington D.C. and New York. In 1940 Safeway operated this 29-passenger Flxible Clipper.

Yellow Coach buses were the choice for the Missouri Pacific Trailways fleet for many years. In 1941, six Yellow Coach Model PD3701 diesel buses were purchased. Missouri Pacific had an extensive network of routes generally coinciding with the Missouri Pacific Railroad routes. Most extensive routes were in Missouri and Arkansas. St. Louis-Kansas City and St. Louis-Little Rock-Houston were important main routes. Isolated routes served the Rio Grande Valley of Texas and another isolated route served the Mississippi River Delta south of New Orleans.

In 1940 Burlington Trailways added 15 Yellow Coach PD 3701 buses. The buses had 35 wide seats and were air-conditioned. Burlington also chose General Motors 6-71 diesel engines for these buses. They were used primarily on Burlington's Chicago-Denver and Chicago-San Francisco routes. *Don Coffin Collection*

ACF-Brill supplied Santa Fe Trailways with many buses in the 1930s, 1940s, and early 1950s. Included was this 29P, a 29-passenger model, in 1940. These buses had 124-horsepower Hall Scott horizontal under-floor gasoline engines and were air-conditioned.

Northern Trailways operated a fleet of ACF 37PB buses on its route between New York and Chicago via Pittsburgh and Cleveland. The buses were acquired in 1941. Northern Trailways was the successor of the Safeway Trailways operation over the same route. Three eastern Trailways companies who felt it was important to preserve a connecting line from New York to Chicago owned the route. Safeway had filed for bankruptcy. Northern later was sold to All-American Bus Lines.

Burlington Trailways began acquiring ACF buses in 1942, when 16 Model 37PBS buses were purchased. After World War II, Burlington standardized on ACF-Brill buses for its long-distance services.

Empire Trailways operated a route between Chicago and Columbus, Ohio, in the early 1940s. In 1941 Ben Kramer and C.J. Villeneuve, who operated DeLuxe Trailways in Illinois, bought Empire. It was merged with Victory Trailways into Indianapolis and Southeastern Trailways in 1947. In 1940 Empire Trailways operated this 36-passenger Fitzjohn Falcon. It had a Hercules gasoline engine in the front.

This unusual bus was pressed into service during the World War II days by Evergreen Trailways of Seattle, Washington. Originally built in 1934, it had a General Motors T23 truck chassis and a Wentworth & Irwin Beaver Tail body. Oregon Motor Stages was the original owner. North Bend Stage Line, which became Evergreen Trailways in 1940, bought this bus in 1938. It was later rebuilt and re-powered with an International engine and finally retired in 1950. *E. E. Arneson Collection*

Bus terminals were built by the various National Trailways Bus System Companies. Tri State Trailways built this impressive bus terminal in Jackson, Mississippi. A similar terminal was in Shreveport, Louisiana.

Burlington Trailways had ten Model PDG 3701 Yellow Coach Silversides buses. The Silversides was a style of bus mainly identified with Greyhound Lines, but other companies like Burlington had them in their fleets. Burlington received these buses in 1941. They were air-conditioned and had diesel power.

Evergreen Trailways was the name given to North Bend Stage Line when the company became a National Trailways Bus System member in July 1940. Later that year Evergreen purchased four Yellow Coach Model PD 2903 buses. These small Yellow Coach buses had General Motors 4-71 in-line diesel engines. The picture was taken when the buses were on a charter trip on Vancouver Island's Malahat Highway. *E. E. Arneson Collection*

This Yellow Coach Model PG 3301 was delivered to Trailways of New England in January 1943. This bus was acquired through the Office of Defense Transportation, which governed bus deliveries during World War II. Trailways of New England became the official name of Blueway Trailways in 1941.

Carolina Trailways began as Carolina Coach Company in 1925. The company joined the National Trailways Bus System in 1940. A year later, two of these P-33 Aerocoach buses were bought. By 1947, 126 Aerocoach buses had been purchased by the company. Most of Carolina Trailways' routes were in North Carolina. During World War II Carolina Trailways served many military sites such as Camp Lee.

During World War II Santa Fe Trailways built this "Victory Liner," a double-deck trailer bus, which could seat 117 passengers. It was used to transport workers to factories producing armaments for the war effort. It was reported that maintenance personnel in Santa Fe Trailways' Wichita shop built the vehicle mostly out of plywood.

Southern Trailways was the result of the combination of Tri State Trailways, Interurban Trailways and Bordelon Trailways. Among the large fleet of buses that were operated was this General Motors PDA 3703. The bus featured a reverse of the traditional dominant crimson and cream paint scheme.

Tri State Trailways of South Dakota was a small, little-known Trailways company. A 1949 timetable revealed that in addition to South Dakota, the company served a few cities in Minnesota and went as far north as Fargo, North Dakota. This photograph of the 25-passenger, post-World War II Flxible Clipper Model 25C147 was taken in front of the Tri State bus depot in Fargo. Tri State had no connections with any other Trailways company. It dropped its membership in Trailways in 1952.

Spartan Coach & Manufacturing Company was formed in 1946 and began building small 21- to 25-passenger buses. Burlington Trailways was one of the large bus companies to operate Spartan buses. In 1947 Burlington bought ten Spartan Model S buses. These small buses had a rear-mounted International Blue Diamond engine. Spartan closed its doors in 1949.

Kaiser Industries built this large articulated bus for Santa Fe Trailways in 1946 after World War II. It is believed this was the first articulated intercity bus built for service in the United States. It has a 6-cylinder Cummins diesel engine located under the floor at the front. The bus was air-conditioned and had torsilastic suspension. Santa Fe and later Continental Trailways operated the bus until 1951 in California.

Many Trailways companies operated buses built by C.D. Beck & Co. The 33-passenger Mainliner series of Beck buses was introduced in 1940. These buses had International Red Diamond engines. Production of Mainliners continued after the war. This Beck Mainliner was in Rio Grande Trailways colors and interestingly; it was the only one in the Rio Grande fleet and was leased. *Don Coffin Collection*

Burlington Trailways bought more than 100 Aerocoach buses between 1945 and 1948. The Aerocoaches were used on many Burlington routes especially in Illinois and Iowa. All of the Aerocoach buses in Burlington colors had 33-passenger capacity. Five of the Aerocoach buses had glass tops and were used for sightseeing in the Black Hills of South Dakota. *Don Coffin Collection.*

24342-1

Virginia Stage Line had a rich history dating back to 1925. As it grew it added other bus companies, particularly Consolidated Bus Company in West Virginia. Most of Virginia Stage Lines' routes were in Virginia, but the acquisition of Consolidated was a westward extension as far as Cincinnati, Ohio. The company became Virginia Trailways in 1938, and in 1966 it was acquired by Transcontinental Bus System (Continental Trailways). After World War II, Virginia Trailways bought a number of ACF-Brill IC-37/41 buses and used them on main line service.

In 1945 Continental Bus System became the name of a large new bus system as the result of the merger of Tri State Trailways and Bowen Trailways. Tri State operated many routes, especially in Louisiana and Mississippi. Bowen's routes were mainly in Texas. Other acquisitions followed, making Continental the nation's second-largest intercity bus company. In 1947 Continental was operating ACF-Brill IC-37/41 buses like the one pictured here. These buses were air-conditioned and had a Hall Scott horizontal under-floor gasoline engine.

In 1949 Continental Trailways had ACF-Brill Motors of Philadelphia design a new bus. The result was this prototype bus which featured a deck-and-a-half design with AM and FM radio, buffet service, and a lavatory. It was called the "Continental." A 267-horsepower Hall Scott gasoline engine powered the bus. No further buses of this type were built. If the bus proved successful, which it did not, 450 would have been ordered by Continental.

Aerocoach buses were very popular among Trailways companies from 1939, when Aerocoach bought the bus manufacturing business of Gar Wood Industries, until 1952, when Aerocoach went out of business. Allentown & Reading Transit Company operated this P46 Aerocoach. This small Trailways member was actually owned by Virginia Trailways of Charlottesville, Virginia.

Missouri Kansas & Oklahoma Trailways (MK & O) was one of the few bus companies that was able to acquire new General Motors PD 3751 Silversides buses. This particular model bus was always considered a Greyhound bus. MK & O's route between St. Louis and Oklahoma City paralleled Greyhound's route. Eventually, MK & O left Trailways and coordinated service with Greyhound. This picture, taken in 1951, is at the Crown Coach Company Bus Terminal in Joplin, Missouri.

Queen City Trailways added 25-passenger Flxible Clipper Model 25 C1-47 to its fleet in 1947. These post-World War II Flxible Clipper buses had a front that was changed from previous models. They continued to have either Buick or Chevrolet engines mounted in the rear. Queen City chose Chevrolet power for this bus.

Tennessee Coach Company remained an independent bus company for many years. It had a strategic route system and had through services in connection with both Greyhound Lines and Trailways Companies. It joined the National Trailways Bus System in 1956. The bus pictured here, a General Motors PDA 3703, carried both the Tennessee Coach Company Lines and Trailways names. It was added to the fleet in 1946.

This C-44 ACF-Brill city bus was operated by Continental Trailways, and had local service between Kansas City and Johnson County suburban area in Kansas. Missouri Pacific Transportation Company originally operated this service. The ACF-Brill C-41 had seats for 44 passengers and was powered by a Hall Scott 707-cubic-inch underfloor gasoline engine.

The Mainliner, a bus built by the C. D. Beck & Company, was operated by a number of Trailways companies, especially after World War II when there was a hurry to replace older buses. The Mainliner had a rear mounted International Red Diamond engine. Baggage was carried in a special section inside the bus at the rear. This Beck was one that Smoky Mountain Trailways had bought and was used on the Smoky Mountain routes in North Carolina and Tennessee.

Carolina Scenic Trailways operated routes mainly in North and South Carolina. The company had joined the National Trailways Bus System in 1940 and provided a valuable link with Trailways companies in the area. In 1949 this General Motors Model PDA 4101 was added to the fleet. This model bus had a General Motors diesel engine. It was reported that a total of 335 of these buses were built for various intercity bus companies.

General Motors began offering 35-foot buses to intercity bus companies in 1948. These buses were the Model PDA 4101. Rio Grande Trailways had ordered six PDA 4101 buses in 1948 and when they were delivered, Rio Grande had become a Continental Trailways division. In 1949, 11 more PDA 4101 buses joined the Rio Grande fleet.

This Model 372 Aerocoach was one of the last ones to be built. It, like previous Aerocoach models, featured an all-welded tubular steel framework. It had seats for 37 passengers, and offered a choice of two gasoline engines or a diesel engine. The Aerocoach 372 pictured here was delivered to De Luxe Trailways in Chicago.

The General Motors PD 4103, built in 1951 and 1952, was popular with several Trailways companies. The PD 4103 pictured here was in service by Continental Southern Lines. The model PD 4103 had a General Motors 6-71 diesel engine. The seating capacity normally was for 37 passengers.

Indianapolis and Southeastern Trailways began as Indianapolis and Southeastern Railroad. Later it became known as Southeastern Trailways and in 1998 Greyhound bought the regular route of the company. Charter service continues under the Southeastern Trailways name. Indianapolis and Southeastern began its bus operation between Indianapolis and Cincinnati. Extensions were made and it had an important Trailways route between Chicago and Knoxville and a branch line between Indianapolis and Louisville. Pictured here is one of ten General Motors Model PD 4102 buses purchased by Indianapolis and Southeastern Trailways in 1950.

The Trailways bus pictured here, a General Motors PDA 3702, was delivered to Missouri Pacific Trailways in 1945. In the 1950s this and a number of other General Motors PDA 3702 buses were refurbished with large side windows and a front normally used on the PD 4103 bus. Missouri Pacific Bus Lines did the work, and when Continental Trailways became the new owner of Missouri Pacific (the name had been changed to Midwest Bus Line), this bus became a Continental Trailways bus.

The General Motors PD 4104 was introduced in 1953. Because of its new styling, safety, performance, and comfort features, it achieved great popularity. Smoky Mountain Trailways was one of the first companies to add this new bus to its fleet. Air suspension was the revolutionary new feature. The exceptionally comfortable riding quality received high praise. Large windows also made the bus appealing to passengers. Smoky Mountain Trailways, with its scenic routes, found the new PD 4104 especially popular.

Continental Trailways was one of many Trailways companies to purchase General Motors PD 4104 buses when they were introduced in 1953. Previously, Trailways companies, including Continental, emphasized ACF-Brill buses, but ACF-Brill discontinued its bus building activity the same year. The new General Motors PD 4104 featured air suspension, a General Motors 671 diesel engine, large picture windows, air conditioning and rest room as an option. It was truly a revolutionary new bus for the industry.

Fitzjohn Body Company built bus bodies and complete buses between 1919 and 1958. The Fitzjohn Road Runner bus was displayed at the National Association of Motor Bus Owners convention in 1954. Either a Cummins JBS-600 150-horsepower diesel engine or a Waukesha gasoline engine could be specified. The bus pictured was for Southern Trailways of Macon, Georgia. Southern Trailways routes operated to Augusta, Columbus, and Americus from the hub at Macon. Fitzjohn closed its doors in 1958.

Safeway Trailways of Washington D.C. added 16 new ACF-Brill IC41A buses in 1951. The IC41A was a bus slightly redesigned from the previous IC41 model. The grill from the front was eliminated and the side windows squared. The IC41A was the last intercity bus model to come from ACF-Brill. After the delivery of this bus to Safeway, about 80 more were built. ACF-Brill bus activity came to an end in 1953. Safeway, in the meantime, ran its new ACF-Brill buses for a number of years on the profitable New York-Washington service.

With two-level buses being popularized in the mid-1950s, the Flxible Corporation presented its Two-Level bus in 1954. It was larger than the popular Flxible Clipper buses of the previous two decades. Improved suspension was also being introduced for buses. The Flxible Two-Level buses featured Torsilastic suspension. Also, the new Flxible had a Cummins J-600 diesel engine. Trailways companies acquired a number of these buses to help offset the end of production of ACF-Brill buses, which were mainline buses for Trailways for many years. *Motor Bus Society*

Queen City Trailways operated extensive bus services throughout the Carolinas and Eastern Tennessee. In 1955, Queen City bought three of these Beck deck-and-a-half buses. These buses were the first and only 40-foot buses built by the C.D. Beck & Company of Sidney, Ohio. These buses had 300-horsepower turbocharged Cummins NHRBS 600 diesel engines.

In 1956 the C. D. Beck & Co. introduced the 9000 Series semi-deck-and-a-half bus. It was a 35-foot model, seated 41 passengers and had a 175-horsepower Cummins JT6B diesel engine. This model was the last series of buses built by Beck before the company was sold to Mack Trucks, Inc. Queen City Trailways purchased several of this model Beck bus.

Continental Trailways wanted a special bus for its long-distance service, which would be distinctive and would have large capacity. Karl Kassbohrer AG, important German bus builder, was contacted, and the prototype "Golden Eagle" bus was built. It led the way to a new generation of luxury buses for Continental Trailways. Although the prototype bus had a German MAN diesel engine, all the 50 additional Golden Eagles acquired from Kassbohrer had General Motors diesel engines. A similar model, the "Silver Eagle," was also built by Kassbohrer at the beginning of deliveries.

Two articulated buses, reported to be among the first to be operated by intercity service in the United States, were delivered to Continental Rocky Mountain Lines in 1957. The buses were built by Karl Kassbohrer AG in Germany and called "Academy Express" buses. They operated between Denver and Pueblo, Colorado, via Colorado Springs, where the United States Airforce Academy is located. These buses had seating capacity of 58 passengers and were powered by a Cummins under-floor engine. Pictured here is one of the buses just arriving by ship from Germany.

In the 1960s, Continental Trailways operated a number of "Five Star Luxury Services" non-stops connecting important cities. A red carpet gave the service a special premium touch as the passengers left the bus or when they were boarding. There was a small galley, and a hostess who traveled on each Five Star bus served beverages and snacks.

Continental Trailways had imported the prototype "Golden Eagle" bus in 1956. Two years later, four articulated "Golden Eagle" buses were acquired from Karl Kassbohrer AG in Germany. These 60-foot buses originally operated the Denver-Colorado Springs-Pueblo route in Colorado. It was one of Continental's "Five Star Luxury Services." Later these large buses were transferred to California for the San Francisco-Los Angeles route. The buses had Rolls Royce diesel engines.

The Continental Trailways bus terminal in Houston, Texas, covered a half-block. It featured a large bus loading area. This picture, taken in 1958, showed a Continental Trailways articulated Golden Eagle bus on display under the canopy. Houston was growing at the time, and new buildings could be seen on both sides of the terminal.

Continental Trailways operated several routes referred to as "Five Star Luxury Services." The Kassbohrer "Golden Eagle" bus is pictured at a Kansas Turnpike Toll Booth. It was on the Five Star service on the Kansas Turnpike between Kansas City and Wichita.

The Flxible Corporation introduced the Hi-level, 37-passenger bus in 1960. It had the passenger seating on one level with considerable space below for baggage. Continental American Trailways operated 20 of the Hi-level buses and called them Clipper Eagles. The engine was the Detroit Diesel 6V71 diesel engine. Torsilastic rubber springs were used for suspension.

Trailways of New England experienced some difficult times in the late 1950s. The Trailways organization, through the Trailways Travel Bureau, took over the ownership of Trailways of New England. Then at the end of 1957, Virginia Trailways and Safeway Trailways bought the company and preserved the important link to the National Trailways Bus System. In 1960, eight of these Flxible Hi-level buses were bought for Trailways of New England routes.

In 1961, after taking delivery of final Eagle buses from Karl Kassbohrer AG in Germany, Continental Trailways set up a bus building plant in Brugge, Belgium and the new company was called Bus and Car. It produced Silver Eagle buses for Continental Trailways, and other Trailways companies, as well as independents. These buses were powered by Detroit Diesel 8V-71N diesel engines.

Posing with Old Ironsides in the Boston Harbor is this 1965 Silver Eagle Model 01 bus of Trailways of New England. There were approximately 40 Silver Eagles in the Trailways of New England fleet. The buses were built in Belgium by the Continental Trailways-owned Bus and Car plant. Trailways of New England routes were mainly between Boston and New York. In 1966 the company, along with Virginia Trailways and Safeway Trailways, became part of Continental Trailways.

Southern Kansas Greyhound Lines, also known as SKG Lines, added this Model 01 Silver Eagle in 1964. SKG Lines was actually half owned by Continental Trailways. Greyhound Lines owned the other half. Note the emblem after the SKG Lines names is a combination of the Greyhound dog and the Santa Fe Trailways emblem. SKG Lines ran between Kansas City, Missouri, and Tulsa, Oklahoma.

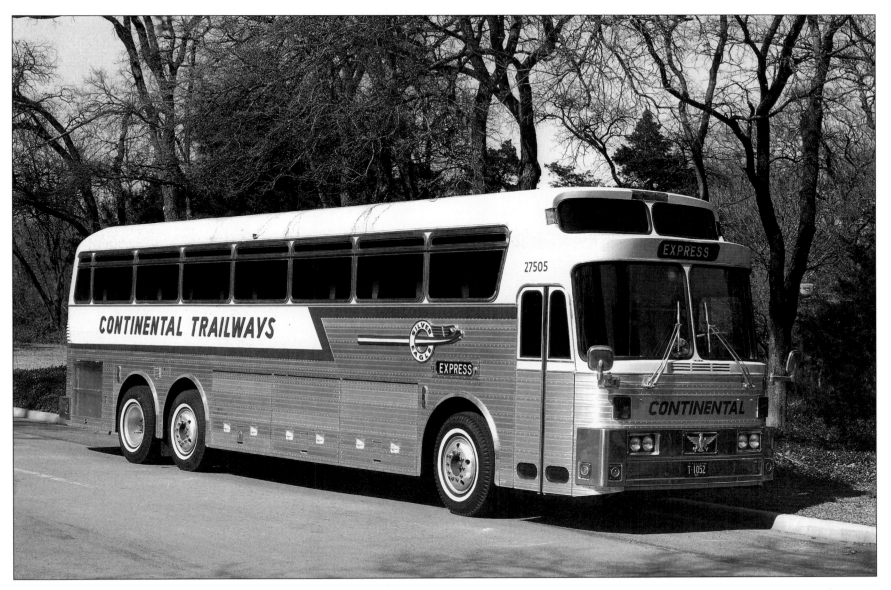

The Model 05 Silver Eagle bus was introduced in 1968. During the building of the Model 05, production of Eagle buses at first was in Belgium, and in the early 1970s, moved to Brownsville, Texas, where Continental Trailways had opened a new bus building factory. Continental Trailways operated many 05 Eagle buses. Other Trailways companies as well as independents bought Model 05 Eagle buses.

A mixture of Silver and Golden Eagle buses are seen in this 1970 picture of Continental Trailways' main maintenance facilities in Dallas, Texas, on Continental Avenue. Dallas was the headquarters for Continental Trailways. The changing Dallas skyline is shown in the distance.

In the 1980s, package express continued to be an important part of the intercity bus business. Some Model 05 Eagle buses were made into combination vehicles with cargo space provided in the rear. Passengers were seated in the front. The bus was operated by Denver, Colorado Springs, Pueblo Motorway of Trailways, Inc.

The production of the Eagle Model 10 bus began in 1980 in Brownsville, Texas, as the Eagle International factory. Continental Trailways, which by that time was known as Trailways, Inc., began adding the new Model 10 bus to its fleet. In addition to the use of the new name the Trailways colors changed from crimson and cream to red and white. The Model 10 had a Detroit Diesel 6-V92TA turbocharged diesel engine. A Model 15 Eagle bus followed the Model 10 in 1985.

Adirondack Trailways became an important member of the National Trailways Bus System in 1940. Its routes were through New York State north from New York City. This General Motors PD 4106 bus was added to the Adirondack fleet in 1962, soon after this model bus was introduced. The Trailways name was predominantly displayed on the bus along with the Trailways slogan, "Easiest Travel on Earth."

Pacific Trailways was the trade name for Mount Hood Stages. This General Motors PD 4106 bus of Pacific Trailways was the last of eight of this model to be bought by Pacific Trailways between 1961 and 1964. These buses were used on a number of Pacific Trailways routes throughout Oregon.

Frank Martz Coach Co., a National Trailways Bus System member since 1936 when the Trailways organization began, purchased this General Motors PD 4106 in 1965. The PD 4106 was the first intercity bus to have the Detroit Diesel 8V-71 diesel engine as standard. It had enough power to operate the air-conditioning system, thereby eliminating the need for a separate engine for air conditioning common with previous buses.

Tamiami Trail Tours began in 1924, but discontinued as an operating company in the early 1930s. It came back in 1935 with routes mainly on Florida's west coast. By 1971, it had routes throughout most of Florida and some service in Georgia as far as Atlanta. Tamiami became a Trailways company in 1940. In 1962 Tamiami Trailways began adding General Motors PD 4106 buses to its fleet.

Western New York Motor Lines was the official name, but when it became a Trailways member in 1962, it became known as Empire State Trailways. In 1972 the name was changed to Empire Trailways. Before becoming a Trailways member it was known as the Blue Bus Line. The main route was between Rochester and Buffalo, New York. Although some local service was operated, especially though Batavia, the New York State Thruway allowed the company an express service. In 1968 Empire Trailways began through service between Buffalo and New York City with Adirondack Trailways. Two of these General Motors PD 4903 buses were bought at that time and assigned to the through service.

Capitol Trailways of Harrisburg, Pennsylvania, bought two General Motors Model S8M 5303A suburban-type buses in 1968 to operate local route in the Harrisburg area. Capital joined the National Trailways Bus System in 1948 and continues to be a member. The Model S8M 5303 A buses were designed for suburban service. They had 8V-71 Detroit Diesel engines.

These three Transportation Manufacturing Corporation (TMC) Model MC-9 buses were part of a delivery of five buses to Carolina Trailways in 1984. Note the stylized three-C logo on the side; Cs which stands for Carolina Coach Company. Carolina has been a Trailways member since 1940. *Don Coffin Collection*

In the 1980s there were a number of new members to the Trailways organization. Michigan Trailways was one of these companies. Prior to joining Trailways in 1981, the company was known as Delta Bus Company and also Valley Coach Lines. These companies were mainly charter companies. When Michigan Trailways began, it operated a route from Bay City, Michigan, to Toledo, Ohio, via Saginaw, Flint, and Ann Arbor. This Motor Coach Industries MC-9 was one of the buses in the Michigan Trailways fleet.

Lakefront Trailways of Cleveland, Ohio, has been a member of Trailways since 1980. The Motor Coach Industries MC-9 bus pictured here joined the Lakefront fleet in 1979. It became an Ohio promotional bus with various cities and areas of Ohio advertised on the side of the bus. In addition to a large charter, tour, and airport service, Lakefront has regular-route services between Buffalo, New York, and Cincinnati, Ohio; Columbus, Ohio, and Chicago; and Charleston, West Virginia, and Baltimore, Maryland.

In 1992 the Spokane, Washington-based Northwestern Stage Lines joined Trailways and became known as Northwestern Trailways. The original route linked Boise, Idaho, with Spokane. In 1992, a new route was started between Spokane, Seattle, and Tacoma. The Motor Coach Industries 102D3 pictured here was added to the fleet at that time. The company owns 25 motorcoaches and, in addition to the regular routes, considerable charter and tour service is operated.

This Motor Coach Industries 102D3 motorcoach is one of ten that joined the Carolina Trailways fleet in 1998. Note the Greyhound dog on the front. Greyhound bought Carolina Trailways in 1997; however, Carolina Trailways retains the red and white Trailways colors and the Trailways name. These Motor Coach Industries motorcoaches in the Carolina Trailways fleet have Detroit Diesel Series 60 4-cycle engines and an Allison World Transmission. Tom Jones Collection

Fullington Auto Bus Company of Clearfield, Pennsylvania, is one of the oldest bus companies in America. Its beginnings date back to 1908 when horse buses were operated. Fullington is a newer Trailways member joining in 1981. The company operates route service, charters, and school bus routes. In the fleet are Motor Coach Industries Model 102C3, two of which are pictured along with the other model Motor Coach Industries motorcoaches.

Burlington Trailways joined Trailways in 1981 when the owners moved from New Jersey to Burlington, Iowa, and acquired the Cedar Rapids, Iowa-St. Louis, Missouri, route from Continental Trailways. In 1997, this Motor Coach Industries 102DL3 bus was purchased. It has a Detroit Diesel Series 60 engine and an Eaton 7-speed transmission. Passenger amenities include six VCR monitors. Burlington has expanded its route service and now has a Chicago-Omaha, Nebraska, and a Davenport, Iowa-Indianapolis, Indiana, route.

One of the largest companies in the Trailways organization is Peter Pan Bus Lines of Springfield, Massachusetts. It has a fleet of 150 motorcoaches, including this 45-foot Motor Coach Industries Model 102DL3. Peter Pan has had a colorful history, with its beginnings dating back to 1933. For many years it operated only in Massachusetts, mainly between Springfield and Boston. More recently, the company expanded to New York and Philadelphia and as far as Washington D.C. The Peter Pan Trailways buses have a traditional green and white Peter Pan color, but the Trailways name and logo are used.

Rimrock Trailways of Billings, Montana, has 39 buses in its fleet. One of the large 45-foot buses in the fleet is this 1998 Motor Coach Industries 102DL3 bus. It has a Series 60 Detroit Diesel engine and a B500 Allison World transmission. Rimrock operates an extensive route service in Western Montana and Idaho, and does considerable charter business. Note the new Trailways global emblems on the front and the side of this bus.

Capitol Trailways of Harrisburg, Pennsylvania, added these two Prevost H3-41 buses to its fleet of 39 buses in 1998. Capital uses these buses for its regular-route service and for charters and tours. One of the most important Capitol routes is through service with other companies between Toronto, Ontario and Washington D.C.

Pine Hill Trailways operates this Motor Coach Industries 96A3 bus with some 25 other buses that are in its fleet. New York State cities on Pine Hill routes include New York City, Kingston, Oneonta, Cooperstown and Utica. Pine Hill Trailways is under the same ownership as Adirondack Trailways and New York Trailways. It joined the Trailways organization with Adirondack in 1940.

Panhandle Trailways of Amarillo, Texas, has 21 buses including this Motor Coach Industries 102D3 bus. It is used with similar buses on a St. Louis-Los Angeles through bus service involving Panhandle's Oklahoma-Amarillo route. Panhandle is also active in the charter and tour market.

Southeastern Trailways of Indianapolis, Indiana, has two of these Motor Coach Industries 102D3 buses for its important charter and tour market. These buses are equipped with video monitors and other luxury refinements for the passengers.

Martz Trailways, Wilkes-Barre, Pennsylvania, has nine Prevost H3-41 buses in its fleet. They were first acquired in 1995. Martz operates a busy daily commuter service between Northern Pennsylvania and New York City's Port Authority Terminal and Wall Street. The Prevost buses are used on this service as well as for charter and tour services operated by Martz. Martz is one of the original Trailways companies.

Western Trailways of Canada operates a regular daily service between Vancouver, British Columbia, and Seattle, Washington, and Sea-Tac Airport. Pictured here is one of the two 1997 Van Hool T-900 coaches in the 17 bus fleet of this Vancouver-based Trailways Company. The company first joined the Trailways organization in 1984.

Orange Belt Stages, Visalia, California, added this Motor Coach Industries Model 102E3 Renaissance coach to its fleet in 1999. This coach is identical to one acquired a year before. It has 54 seats, six video monitors, and other passenger refinements. Orange Belt States has been in business since 1934 and a Trailways member since 1997. It operates a route service in California's Central Valley and also operates extensive charter and tour service.

This Prevost Model H3-45 and one other were added to the Burlington Trailways fleet in 1998 and 1999. The Prevost pictured here has a Detroit Diesel Series 60 engine and an Eaton 10-speed Autoshift. It seats 54 passengers, and has a galley and VCR monitors. Burlington, headquartered in West Burlington, Iowa, has a number of regular service routes through the Midwest and does considerable charter and tour service.

The Martz Group of Wilkes-Barre, Pennsylvania, has eight divisions in the East from New York to Florida. One company in the group is Martz Trailways, the only remaining founding Trailways company. Martz Trailways operates considerable route service between northeastern Pennsylvania and New York City as well as serving Scranton, Wilkes-Barre and Philadelphia. Martz acquired this Motor Coach Industries 102E3 Renaissance bus in 1999, adding to the approximately 400 other buses in the Group.

Adirondack Trailways of Kingston, New York, has an extensive route system through New York State. One of its most important routes is between Albany and New York City. Adirondack owns two other Trailways companies, Pine Hill Trailways and New York Trailways. Adirondack became a National Trailways Bus System member in 1940. Since 1995, Adirondack has added 18 Prevost motorcoaches to its fleet, including the H3-41 pictured here. Four of the new Prevost motorcoaches are lift equipped.

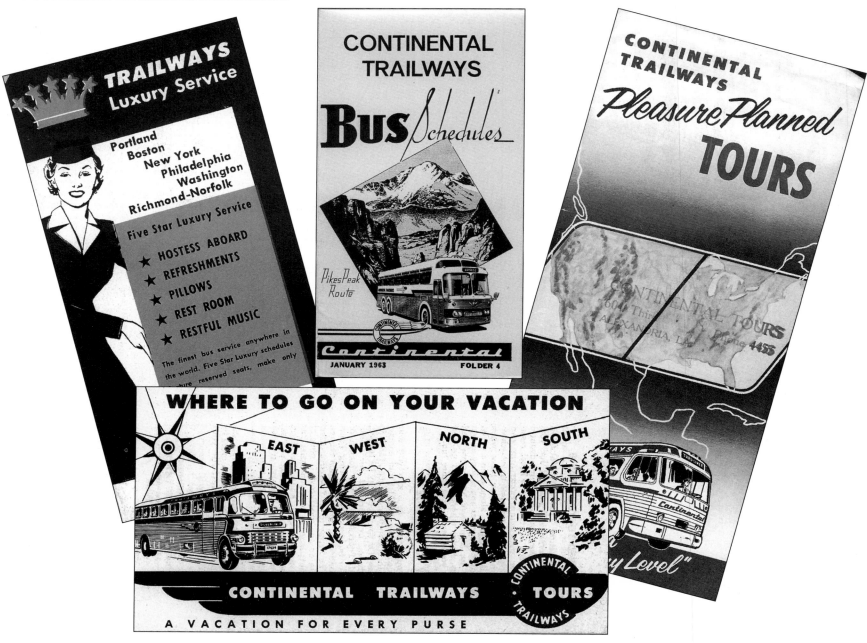

SEE AMERICA at *Scenery Level!*

GULF COAST U.S.A.

TRAILWAYS TOU[...]
SHREVEPORT, LA[...]
PHONE 3-4207 P. O. B[...]

TRAILWAYS *Serves the Nation*

To Really Travel...Go **TRAILWAYS**

at "Scenery Level"

- luxury travel at the lowest cost
- clean, comfortable, restful coaches
- pleasure planned tours everywhere
- frequent schedules for your convenience
- faithfully serving the entire nation

NATIONAL **TRAILWAYS** BUS SYSTEM

CONTINENTAL TRAILWAYS
DELUXE ESCORTED TOUR TO
FLORIDA AND THE **DEEP SOUTH**
SPRING FLOWER TOUR

from SALT LAKE CITY

CONTINENTAL TRAILWAYS

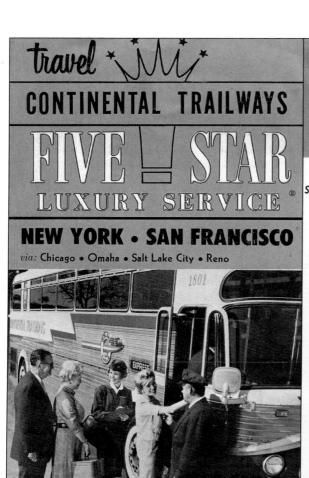

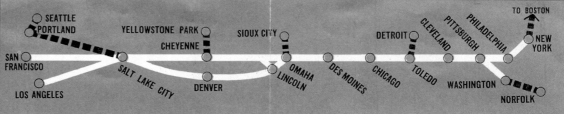

CONTINENTAL TRAILWAYS NEW THRU BUS SERVICE COAST TO COAST

SUPERB SILVER EAGLE SERVICE — *Golden Nugget route* FIVE-STAR LUXURY SERVICE! ®

Dark Figures P.M. — Light Figures A.M.

READ DOWN																				READ UP					
♛ *5 00	6 00	*1100	*3 59			7 00	6 00			12 30	Lv Boston, Mass. ....(EST) (7180) (TNE)	Ar		2 45	2 45	3 15		8 29		11 29	
*9 59	10 59					12 29	1138			5 15	Ar New York, N.Y. ....(7180) (TNE)	Lv	♛	9 30	9 30	10 30		3 30		5 30	
*1100	12 30	Exp	1 00			2 00	1230			*9 30	Lv New York, N.Y. ....(R) (CTS)	Ar	Exp	*7 50	8 50	9 25		3 10		3 20	
1 05	6 29		7 00			2 15	3 05			*1135	Lv Philadelphia, Pa. ....(R) (8008)	Ar		*1245	11 35	12 25		12 45		1 00	
*3 15	7 45		10 15			2 15	3 35			*1 45	Lv Harrisburg, Pa.	Ar			12 25	12 40		10 15		10 45	
*7 05			2 15			9 15	9 25			*5 30	Ar Pittsburgh, Pa. ....(CTS)	Lv						6 15		6 55	
6 30			2 30			7 00	1 45				Lv Norfolk, Va. ....(7310) (CCC)	Ar		11 35	1 30			7 45		10 15	
9 45			5 15			9 45	4 00				Lv Richmond, Va. ....(7252) (VaT)	Ar		8 45	10 45			3 45		4 30	
1 00			8 00			2 15	10 15				Lv Washington, D.C. ....(CTS)	Ar		7 30	9 30			1 10		1 45	
1 50			8 50			3 05	11 00				Lv Baltimore, Md. ....(8010)	Ar		6 25	6 25			1205		1 15	
*8 15			2 30				5 00				Lv Pittsburgh, Pa.	Ar		12 01	12 01			6 30		7 30	
1115			3 15		10 15	1 00	6 00				Ar Pittsburgh, Pa. ....(CTS)	Lv		*1145		11 40		5 15		5 55	
1 45			8 00		1 30	6 30	8 45				Ar Cleveland, Ohio ....(8008)	Lv		6 30		8 30		1 20		1 15	
			11 30		4 30	8 15	11 00				Ar Toledo, Ohio	Lv				6 15					
2 35					10 25					12 50	Lv Toledo, Ohio ....(8004)	Ar		5 50		6 05		1025		1 16	1150
8 00					11 45					2 15	Ar Detroit, Mich. ....(8004)	Lv		4 30		4 45		9 25		1 00	
11 50										9 00	Lv Detroit, Mich. ....(8004)	Ar		7 30				1230		10 45	
1 10										10 25	Ar Toledo, Ohio ....(8004)	Lv		6 15				1230		2 35	
*2 00			10 35			3 20	11 15				Lv Toledo, Ohio ....(EST) (8008)	Ar		6 15		10 40					
5 45			2 40			7 00	2 30				Ar Chicago, Ill. ....(CST)	Lv		*1225		11 15					
*7 00											Lv Chicago, Ill.	Ar		*1125		11 15		5 45		5 45	
*7 105			8 00			9 00					Aurora, Ill.			To		9 30		4 45		4 45	
1135			9 00			2 15					Lv Burlington, Ia. ....(8012)	Ar		Peoria							
			10 05		7 00	3 40					Lv Ottumwa, Ia.			9 20							
			11 20		6 10	12 15					Lv Rock Island, Ill.			7 10							
*7 10			6 30		10 10	12 45					Ar Davenport, Ia.	Lv		7 35		1 30					
*7 30			4 20		11 45	1 31					Ar Muscatine, Ia.	Lv			9 15			2 45		2 35	
*9 00			8 15	10 30	11 15	5 00					Ar Des Moines, Ia.	Lv		*1201				4 30		4 00	
*1010	9 40		12 05	1 50		x5 15					Lv Omaha, Nebr.	Ar		*1055		8 35		3 35		2 25	
f	10 10					x6 00					Lv Omaha, Nebr. ....(8015) (8018)	Ar		7 20		6 45		3 10		2 15	
10 55						x7 45					Lv Lincoln, Nebr.	Lv		5 30		6 45		9 30		1 30	
*1230						x6 45					Lv Hastings, Nebr.	Lv		*6 40				9 48		1 10	
1 30						x8 45					Seward, Nebr.			*6 40		7 30		9 45		1 00	
2 15						x9 00					York, Nebr.			*6 40		4 30		9 40		1 00	
3 00						x6 45					Lv Grand Island, Nebr.	Lv		*6 40		f		9 30		12 10	
5 05						10 35					Kearney, Nebr.			*6 10		4 10		8 10		11 30	
*7 15						11 35					Lexington, Nebr.			*6 15		10 40		7 35		11 10	
*1052						11 45					Ar North Platte, Nebr. ....(CST)	Lv		*6 05		10 00		6 15		11 00	
x1 00						11 45					Ogallala, Nebr. ....(MST)			*6 05		8 00					
8 15											Ar Sidney, Nebr.	Lv									
9 30											Ar Cheyenne, Wyo.	Lv									
11 30			9 20		10 20	x1 37					Ar Denver, Colo.	Lv		8 00		x1 00		8 25		x1205	
1 30			10 45		11 20	x1 37					Lv Denver, Colo.	Ar		7 30		x1052		6 50		x5 52	
2 05			11 30			4 25					Lv Cheyenne, Wyo.	Ar		*1050		x1 00		8 35		x1205	
3 40			12 15			4 25					Laramie, Wyo.			*9 45		6 10		8 10			
5 25			12 45			6 30					Rawlins, Wyo.			*9 00		5 20		7 15			
7 50			3 05			8 35					Rock Springs, Wyo.			*7 55		4 50		5 15			
8 05			4 20			9 35					Evanston, Wyo.			*7 55		9 20		4 15			
9 45			5 05			10 20					Ar Ogden, Utah	Lv		*7 00		8 50		1 45			
7 15			4 25			11 10					Ar Salt Lake City, Utah	Lv		6 00		8 30		1 15			
x1052			2 10	11 40		1 37					Lv Salt Lake City, Utah ....(MST)	Ar		*1215		5 30		10 30		1205	
x1 00			6 05	4 15		x5 52					Lv Elko, Nev. ....(PST)	Lv		*6 40		11 45		9 20		2 25	
8 15			1 30	4 35							Lv Winnemucca, Nev.	Lv		*6 40		11 45		8 15		1 40	
9 30			10 25	3 35							Lovelock, Nev.			7 55		7 55		8 05		1 30	
11 30			12 15	10 10							Ar Reno, Nev.	Lv		7 15		7 15		7 45		1 15	
3 40			3 05	1 30		3 05					Ar Sacramento, Cal. ....(R)	Lv		*4 45		1 45		6 15			
4 45			4 00	3 20		4 20					Vallejo, Cal. ....(R)			*4 30		1 25		6 30			
5 05			4 00	3 20		4 20					Oakland, Cal. ....(R)			12 25		1 20		4 55			
x1010			4 25	4 25		4 25					Ar San Francisco, Cal. ....(PST) (CTS)	Lv		*8 00		12 01		4 00			
			1 40	12 01	12 01		1 40				Lv Salt Lake City, Utah ....(MST)	Ar				6 00		12 35		12 35	
			4 45	5 20	5 20		4 55				Lv Cedar City, Utah	Lv				12 43		6 45		6 45	
			10 45	7 55	7 55		10 45				Lv Las Vegas, Nev. ....(PST)	Lv				12 43		1 25		1 25	
			3 50	1 35	1 35		3 50				Lv San Bernardino, Cal. ....(R)	Lv				7 55		6 45		6 45	
			5 40	3 45	3 45		5 40				Lv Los Angeles, Cal. ....(R)	Lv				12 45		7 00		7 00	
			7 30	7 40	7 40		7 30				Lv Los Angeles, Cal.	Ar				11 35	11 55	6 00		6 00	
			8 37	8 40	8 40						Ar Long Beach, Cal.	Lv				10 48	10 48	4 55		4 55	
			11 30	11 30	11 30		11 30				Ar San Diego, Cal. ....(PST)	Lv				8 05		4 00		4 00	
8 30			2 15	1 00	1 00		2 15			11 00	Lv Salt Lake City, Utah ....(MST) (PT)	Ar	11 00				2 15		3 05	
9 25			3 15	1 55	1 55		3 15			9 50	Lv Ogden, Utah ....(7942)	Lv	9 50			7 30			7 00	
6 05			5 50	9 40	9 40		11 20			1 15	Ar Boise, Idaho ....(MST)	Lv	1 15			1220			7 00	
2 30			9 50	9 50	9 50		9 50			11 15	Ar Portland, Ore. ....(PST) (PT)	Lv	11 15			1145			6 15	
			2 30	2 15	2 15		2 30			5 00	Ar Seattle, Wash. ....(8560) (PST) (CTS)	Lv	5 00			7 00			1 30	

(CST)—Central Standard Time. (EDT)—Eastern Daylight Time. (EST)—Eastern Standard Time. (MST)—Mountain Standard Time. (PST)—Pacific Standard Time.

Silver Eagle®. Golden Eagle®.

(VaT)—Virginia Trailways.
■—Restroom equipped bus.
♦—By connection.
(CD)—Only except Sundays and Holidays.
(CD)—Daily except through time.
■—Reserved seat arrangements from these points to first transfer or bus change point.

(CTS)—Continental Trailways. (CCC)—Carolina Trailways. (PPT)—Pacific Trailways. (STs)—Safeway Trailways. (TNE)—Trailways of New England. (R)—Five Star Luxury Service.

♛ or *—Five Star Luxury Service® (Extra Fare).

All trips operate daily unless otherwise noted.

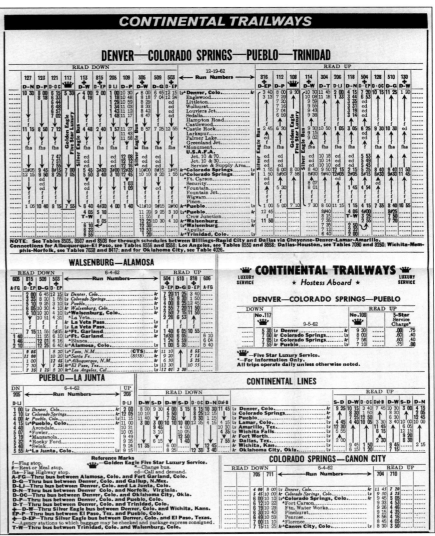

A Word from the Author

I have enjoyed being involved in the bus industry for more than 50 years. Not only has bus transportation been my vocation, it has also been my avocation. The history, development, and growth of the bus industry have fascinated me.

I have collected considerable bus history information. My library has many books, trade journals, reports, timetables, and a large selection of bus photographs, many of which appear in this photo archive book.

My first encounters with Trailways were through studying timetables of the various Trailways member companies in issues of Russells Official Bus Guide. I also began reading about Trailways buses and their operating procedures.

Over the years, I have traveled many miles on Trailways buses. My first experiences were while serving in the army. Among some of the trips I took were on Missouri Pacific Trailways buses in Arkansas. Then in Virginia and North Carolina, I rode ACF buses of Carolina and Virginia Trailways. I also recall riding an Aerocoach Model EFI of Virginia Trailways between Richmond and Charlottesville.

In the years that followed, I rode more ACFs, Yellow Coaches, Flxibles, Aerocoaches, MCIs, Prevosts, and other bus types carrying the Trailways name.

During my career in the bus industry, I met many wonderful people in the Trailways organization. One of the Trailways pioneers I had the pleasure of knowing was I. B. James of Burlington Trailways fame.

In addition I have established other friendships with bus people from many bus companies, transit systems and related companies, not only the United States and Canada but around the world.

The bus industry has been, and still is, a rewarding experience for my wife and myself.

William A. Luke
3/2/00

MORE TITLES FROM ICONOGRAFIX:

This product is sold under license from Mack Trucks, Inc. Mack is a registered Trademark of Mack Trucks, Inc. All rights reserved.

All Iconografix books are available from direct mail specialty book dealers and bookstores worldwide, or can be ordered from the publisher. For book trade and distribution information or to add your name to our mailing list and receive a **FREE CATALOG** contact:

Iconografix, PO Box 446, Hudson, Wisconsin, 54016   Telephone: (715) 381-9755, (800) 289-3504 (USA), Fax: (715) 381-9756

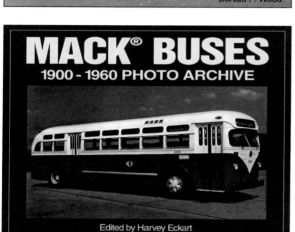

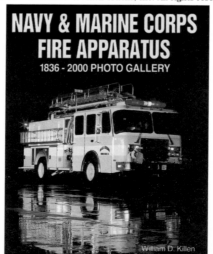
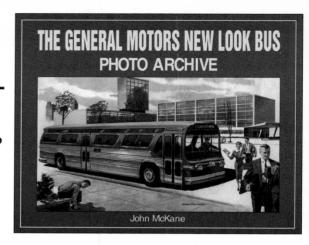
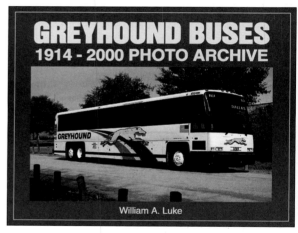
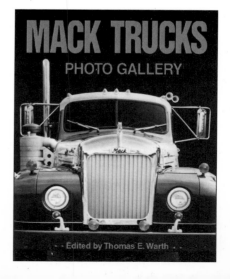